Paradise, Indiana

Bruce Snider

Paradise, Indiana

PLEIADES
PRESS

Lena-Miles Wever Todd Poetry Series

Warrensburg, Missouri

Department of English
University of Central Missouri
Warrensburg, Missouri 64093

Distributed by Louisiana State University Press

Cover Image: *MEXICO. 1994. La Batea. Zacatecas. Mennonites.*
Copyright © Larry Towell/ Magnum Photos. Used with the permission of Magnum Photos.

Book design by Wayne Miller. Author's photo by Lysley Tenorio.

2 4 6 8 9 7 5 3 1
First Pleiades Press Printing, 2012

Financial support for this project has been provided by a UCM Foundation Opportunity Grant, the Missouri Arts Council, a state agency, and the National Endowment for the Arts.

To my father and mother, Bruce and Kay Snider

And in memory of C. B. and J. S.

Contents

Bequeath us to no earthly shore until
Is answered in the vortex of our grave
The seal's wide spindrift gaze toward paradise.

—Hart Crane, "Voyages"

Map

There ought to be a fire somewhere in Indiana,
not this night across the fields in Indiana.

And God said let there be light, and there was light.
And God said let there be corn, and there was Indiana.

I kiss my love, taking his hand near the deer stand.
Honey is fragrant on the table, and there is thunder in Indiana.

And what of Amy Blaine, who drowned when she was twelve?
Nights, I feel her in the cold rain of Indiana.

For the rest of my life I'll feel the wet hair plastered to her face.
I'll feel darkness, and the magpie's feathers in Indiana.

But I'm not interested in grief, just the sound of the yellowthroat,
just the warblers in the thickets of Muncie, Indiana.

I don't need a communion wafer.
I need the autumn mist of Indiana.

Arcola, Goshen, Nappanee. Remember a place where the river bank
passes through you, where the Amish girls spread their skirts in Indiana.

Remember a place where spring breaks the yellow news of the pawpaw tree,
where a pan of grease hisses against a flame called Indiana.

Lord, the boys touch other boys, eating fried dough
and glazed apples, lips sticky with syrup and heat in Indiana.

Each winter, sleet turns the cornfield into a cemetery.
Its epitaph reads: Indiana.

My father's pulse slows between systole and diastole,
between the frozen creek beds and the grain silos of Indiana.

And you will ask: Where are the lilacs?
And I will answer: Under the snows of Indiana.

Soon, spring buds will thrust their sex organs into the mouths of bees.
Their story is the story of Indiana.

If there are a hundred ways to recall the dogwood in bloom,
this is the one where your parents make love on a battered sofa in Indiana.

Stamen and pistol, pollen in the air, the field of poppies knows lust
spells its name: I-N-D-I-A-N-A.

What's death, after all, if not the Wabash wearing down river stones,
if not the muskrat flicking its damp tail in Indiana?

Are those angels' trumpets? Is that God calling
Bruce? Have I reached the end of the world? Or Indiana?

Epitaph

Because I could be written anywhere,
I loved the hard surface of the blade,
my name carved into barn doors, desktops,
the peeled face of a shag-bark hickory.
I pressed my whole weight into it, letters

grooved deep as the empty
field rows along Tri-Lakes where I'd seen
my cousin Nick buried in ground so hard
they had to heat the dirt with lamps
before they could dig. I gutted squirrels

my grandmother fried, hanging
skins from the window,
and with the same knife gouged a B
at the base of the frozen creek bank,
the season breaking

like the rose our teacher, Miss Jane,
dipped in nitrogen so it would shatter.
There were more atoms, she claimed,
in the letter O, than people in the entire state.
I could feel God inside that letter,

the vast sky refigured, buds scrawled
on the black limbs of trees.
Trucks carried spring feed down
Highway 9 as I wove through headstones,
tracing names in the late frost,

looking for Nick's plot
with the wax white roses,
his lucky fishing lure. I could sense
him down there, satin-lined,
curled like the six-toed cat

we'd found bloated in the creek,
alive with lice and maggots. Sometimes
I was sure I could hear him, restless,
waiting for me, the Wabash
pushing its icy waters, my tongue

humming with the fizz. It never ended,
that stretch of road snaking back home
like an artery through my own heart
where an owl gripped a rat in its claw
over I-80. I'd put my hands in my pockets

and walk, dreaming of the places I'd go,
the things I'd do, the dump rising
to meet me at the edge of town,
chrome bumpers twisted as the owner
himself, withered arm swinging a fist.

I waited for something to escape—
mouse darting from a glove box, oil
from a cracked sump. I could stand
on a crushed Chevy, feeling it all
thaw inside me: asphalt

and barbed wire, cows and steaming
pails of milk, even the graveyard
rising, new stones nursing old griefs,
slow bones and winter's cherry trees
making their long walk to leaf.

At These Speeds

for Nick 1971-1988

He saved for months (mowing lawns, taking
    extra shifts at the Dairy Queen) and when

finally he brought it home, I helped him
    swirling rags, polishing until the hubcaps shone,

the tires special ordered to fit. *Easy ride*, he'd say,
    slamming the brakes—his big joke—instrument panel

lighting the glove box filled with the manual's
    sweet talk—*fuel injector, carburetor, exhaust*

manifold. So when the call came, I couldn't
    help but wonder if he'd planned it all along—

the shut garage, engine idling, sunglasses
    slung from the mirror. On the passenger's side

a school book lay open; chewed gum on the seat.
    For months I pictured each moment before

and after the men left, the sirens faded,
    the car now parked, sitting motionless,

a proud animal crouched in the long grass
    as if it knew, one day, it would take me, too,

driving into some starless night, leather cold
    against my skin. But how could I imagine

such travel, knowing only the grief of it,
    which held me as it must have held him, engine

quivering, headlights filling the dark ordinary
    garage, one sudden brilliance, then the next?

Afterlife

The cold day grinds like a starter
that won't turn over, key gripped

in my hand. I wake hard
with another dream of him, arms

pulling me into the shanty, gooseflesh
against mosquito welts, his tongue

salty in my mouth. Cold shower
and dry toast. I hike the back

woods, cut limbs from shore pine.
In the chicken coop, a red fox filches

eggs, tensing its jaw, light wagging
in black limbs, a new word for hunger.

I sit on the porch swing, imagine
the garage opening to a car,

its dark heart filling with exhaust.
Why not admit I don't know

what we become? By the pier: the ice
shanty rusts, tin roof caving, palm prints

on cracked glass. Inside I find his
hockey stick, check the forgotten

trap he set: no rat, no shadow
of a rat. Just skin and guts.

At the Midwest Taxidermy Convention

As if stunned to have entered the gymnasium's cold light,
    the animals stare back, having felt the shape

that love can take, the belts and pulleys
    of the fleshing machine, the mallard's cracked eyes

glittering with disbelief, acrylic moons setting over
    the buffalo's meaty haunches. Here, the lion kneels

beside the lamb, who mothers her own stasis,
    a small ewe sucking her vinyl teat. An embryonic sow,

slick with what it can't bear, floats in blue resin,
    the whitetail deer witness to the antelope fixed

by upholstery nails, a spectral owl trawling
    its strangle of branches. Not even the trays

of teeth disturb them, the waxen tongues,
    the acetone's carnal spray fogging the back room

as the shy beasts look out past the men who made them
    possible, fitting the soft crush of foam in each chest,

hearts perfected by absence, catgut stitches,
    the invisible scars. A little salt preserves

what will never be, such shine to the sparrow's feathers,
    lacquered beak carved with chisel and awl, nylon

cinching the black hawk, silence aloft in its claw.

Romance

1.

Grandma creams butter, tends
the crippled chicken in the cardboard box.

They nearly pecked it to death. Nick and I
wrestle, practice the Tomahawk Chop

and the Indian Death Lock, her
stuffed pet squirrel looking past us

to Roosevelt on the wall, to her shelf
of romance novels—*Tender Midnight, Passion's*

Daughter, Love Evermore. In the sink,
a gutted pig sags, its back flank sliced

for beans and noodles. She moves
hymnals, a wedding photo: Grandma

in her one good dress, Grandpa
square-jawed in his Sunday suit. *He was*

so handsome back then. Her government
check tucked in her Bible, she hands

me one bullet: *Go get me a rabbit.*

2.

In the back acre, we pick apples
throw them one by one. I miss.

Nick: *You couldn't find your ass*
with both hands and a banjo. The asthma

comes; his Adam's apple swims.
Inhaler in hand, he turns, his breath

the parakeet's molting dust. In the coop,
we freshen a fouled pan. I love

the smell of gasoline when, shirtless,
he drives the combine. In a pasture

staked nearby, the new Guernsey
catches Little Girl's scent. Aroused,

it pushes hard. We watch the bull
lick her, its jerky mounting.

It snorts. White semen strings
run the udder's length. Grandpa,

smiling, slaps her flank: *Bullseye.*

Late Harvest

It isn't summer
that goes on forever, but the fall—
stacks of gourds collapsing,

warm water turned tepid overnight.
Nick's the first to sign
my plaster cast, his girlfriend

by his side, my leg propped
on a pillow we shared as boys
that winter of fever and pox.

Inking a small heart,
she signs, too, right over the break.
I imagine the swing of hips

on his blue bedspread, her bikini
top falling fast. A week later,
he takes my arm when we stand

alone, listening to steer calve
one barn down, hens dumbstruck
in their cages. Against a tree,

he unzips my fly, a crush
of apples overhead where
gnats swarm about

the bruised ones that come
apart so quickly when
you put them in your mouth.

Planetary

for Miss Jane 1953-2007

Today they lowered you, shovels
charting your descent as you once
charted the solar system, strips of dark
blue crepe and glue sticks, yellow
construction paper for Saturn's rings.

The temperature of the moon,
you said, varied on its sunlit side,
a comet's tail not a tail at all, just a ribbon
of fiery ice. Leaning over my desk,
you smelled of drugstore perfume

and moisturizer, your hair a stunning
peroxide blonde, as you told me about
Ham, the Astrochimp, who rode a shuttle
to the stars, then died eating an apple
in his cage. At the planetarium,

you stepped off the bus, your face,
even then it seems, composed
of memory and the same compounds
that make up a distant star: hydrogen,
carbon, ash. For years I remembered

how a giant sun spends the last days
of its life forging an iron heart,
transmuting hydrogen into helium,
oxygen into silicon. How to master
such a feat, willing oneself to metal?

Even the telescope couldn't explain
everything, its lens making the whole sky
blaze as you stood in your lime silk blouse,
poised to take the next step and the next,
satellites passing overhead like theories

of the soul. The truth is most meteors burn
out, smaller than drops of water, hurled by
friction to dust. If you were here, you might
explain how each minute
photons from a great supernova

are tearing towards us, moving
through the Oort cloud, its cemetery
of icy bodies. You'd say not even
light can penetrate the deepest recesses
of space, that time and distance

are always relative, that outside,
even now, people pass under some dead
star's flicker, so much taken on faith, grief
and the moon's dry filament forged
in the still dark spaces between the trees.

Chemistry

Chemicals filled the air outside
       the rubber hose plant where I'd bike
past the trail ruts by the pond,
       leaves shivering outside
the funeral home where Mr. Debb,
       the mortician, wiped down caskets
with his smooth clean hands, his nails
       perfectly trimmed. He lived
with a younger man—That Mexican,
       my father called him—in a house
along the river. In the summer
       we'd egg the windows, bright yolks
spattering blue siding. *Up The Ass,*
       Nick wrote with Aunt Starr's
lipstick, spiking the flower bed
       with tampons. Once, pedaling past,
I saw the Mexican, shirtless,
       cutting the grass, something in me
rising explosive as my parakeet bursting
       from its cage, wings a yellow span
of barbs and barbules. When I came
       across a dead raccoon, I peeled back,
with a pen-knife, the viscera
       as I might peel a grape, its secrets
stored in a small vial from my chemistry set:
       gelatinous, the faint marbling of muscle.
Even the buckeyes I picked
       along the dirt road opened
to soft grey meat, so much hidden
       where you'd least expect it
like the finger Ben Jennings swore
       his brother found in a Pepsi can.
I imagined it floating, jagged nail
       nudging the rim. At dusk
lights shone from the back rooms

of the funeral home where the dead
lay stretched on tables, night
unraveling like black thread
used to sew their mouths shut.

Indiana History

Another field trip to the Old Fort, photos of pioneer women, fingers
    blackened by cold.

Mr. Webber says: *Research your family heritage.*

That sonuvabitch: Grandma's voice slurred in snot and tears.

She stands against the window, swollen eye barely open over her
    split cheek.

Is it me who pushes Tim Franklin on the stairs?

Is it me who calls him *pussy* when he cries?

I take notes, memorize the answers.

At night, in the kitchen, Nick presses hard against me when no one
    else can hear.

Never touch a dead cat, she says.

Never wake Grandpa when he's been out all night.

*By 1943 women constitute one-third of the factory workers in
    Indiana.*

Midnight, drunk again, Grandpa knocks the door. *Come out,* he slurs,
    or I'm coming in.

The projector sticks. Mr. Webber runs it backwards.

Always Nick's mouth on mine, my back against the cold linoleum.

Always through the bedroom wall, I hear her crying.

Another photo of a bonneted woman stirring a big pot in the hearth.

25% of Hoosier women died, their long dresses and aprons
catching fire.

How does he say he's sorry? Why does she take him back?

I take the test but don't know the answers.

Nick rolls over, climbs on top: *Now you be the girl.*

Afterlife

I wake to leafless vines and muddy fields,
patches of standing water. His pocketknife

waits in my dresser drawer, still able to gut fish.
I pick up his green shirt, put it on for the fourth day

in a row. Outside, the rusty nail he hammered
catches me, leaves its stain on everything.

The temperature drops, the whole shore
filling with him: his dented chew can, waders,

the cattails kinked, bowing their distress.
At the pier, I use his old pliers to ready the line:

fatheads, darters, a blood worm jig. Today, the lake's
one truth is hardness. When the trout bite,

I pull the serviceable things glistening into air.

My Grandmother Shoplifting at the Pick 'n Save

Because her hands are chapped from raking
she tucks a pair of gloves beside the coffee
mug in her coat. Aisle by aisle, she's drawn
by the gleaming racks of glass, the strange

melancholy of dish detergent. She takes
what she needs and what she doesn't—
metal pail, deck of cards—a small meanness
filling her. Some days she dreams her sons:

the oldest outside Millford, the pipe-fitter
in Des Moines, their faces reflected in the dead
brilliance of floor cleaner. A stock boy nods
as she pockets a Christ Church pamphlet

from a stack near the register. She thinks
of the day she found her sister drowned
in Millford's pond, limp body on the bank
in a red-checked hand-me-down

dress—such a hot July and all those people
at their picnics, their blank faces rising
before her even now as she brushes against
a blue ash tray, palms a tobacco tin, moves

past stacks of bath mats and towels.
Nothing can stop her as she steps
toward the open exit, rain breaking the hack-
berry's sluggish thorns. She can smell

the nearby creek as if it were streaming through her,
mix of pine pitch and thistle. She knows
it's fed by the underground springs of Kosciusko.
She knows the waters beneath run cold.

Tornado Season

On my knees in the gymnasium, I pictured
        my mother's jewelry box, my father's
fishing rod, the mobile home park
               in Nappanee swept away. I envied
the missing still lost in the storm,
        licked clean by wind, faults torn away
like shredded wood and insulation.
               I wanted to see my uncle's farm
from above, grain silo doors akimbo,
        lavender spitting blooms along the fence.
I wanted to see train tracks buckle,
               nail-driven straws of wheat. I wanted
to make the sound the wind made,
        black eye of the storm peering into
me, the funnel cloud as it swirled.
               I wanted to be carried—
green sky, sudden hail—with everything
        I knew: blue spruce, white pine, the grey-
shingled barns of Whitley County, face
               of the barber with his sharpened razor,
Marie at the Waffle House, Beau
        Tucker over mufflers in his shop. I could
sense them all, faithful and faithless
               passing overhead with car doors
and street signs, with stone angels
        from the steps of the Catholic church
last seen cracked down the middle
               as they disappeared over burning fields.

A Great Whirring

My neighbor lifts   a basket of laundry
drapes a white blouse   I envy the way it hangs
empty   un-tethered   My father
once took me to a bee farm   pointing out clover
wheat straw   tarpaper rooflines   bees
body to body   a great whirring
combing the wet cells   Now he forgets
names   calls this morning to say he can't see
the finches at the feeder   nothing
but a faint rustling   watery daubs
of black and gold   All day   I think of him
the hovering birds   breaking seeds   unseen
feeding   the bees knotted together   soft thorax
and stinger   How quickly
things darken this heat   Shadows
split the maple   Kneeling on the lawn
I deadhead roses   With a penknife
cut raw white pulp   sun on the sound
of leaves   rustling brief need
which could be the wind   or his voice
as it passes   headed nowhere   gaining speed

The Drag Queen Dies in New Castle

Returning home
   at twenty-nine, you made
a bed your throne, your
   brothers carrying you
from room to room,

each one in turn holding
   the glass to your lips,
though you were the oldest
   of the brood. Buried
by the barn, you vanished,

but the church women
   bought your wigs
for the Christmas pageant
   that year, your blouses sewn
into a quilt under which

two newlyweds lay,
   skin to skin as if they
carried some sense
   of your undressing. Skirts
swayed where sheep grazed

the plow and the farmer
   reached between legs
to pull out the calf,
   fluid gushing to his feet.
On lines across town,

dresses flapped empty
   over mulch while you
kept putting on your show,
   bones undressing like
it's never over, throwing

off your last great shift
    where a fox snake sank
its teeth into a corn
    toad's back, the whole
field flush with clover.

Parts

In the back of that car, all elbows
and mouths, we knew nothing

corrupted like happiness. We ducked
deeper into ripped seats, two boys

in the shadows of cotton woods:
his freckled back, my bare knees.

Finished, we hit the gas, pistons
grinding, hearts thumping. Dumb

and trusting, we gunned off. And so
when the fan belt snapped,

we junked one from the yard—
spark plug, piston ring—the sinking

engine stripped as if anything
could be saved. What was left

to grieve? We spent hours without
thinking of how the wrecked

cars enter, and how they leave.

Morning After the Monster Truck and Thrill Show

Across the field, ruts open
where trucks—*Maximum*

Destruction, Gravedigger—
gouged tracks in dirt,

black gashes scrawling
the crash of shocks

and struts, fender cleaved
like bone from the face

of the chassis, shorn
steel and splintered glass.

The trucks have passed
into Akron, Indiana.

For the rye grass
it's another day

of rebuilding, the dark
flies lazy on cows, acorn

trees dropping their
wormy meat on rain-

beaten fields where
the tractor plows.

At Floyd's Tuxedo Shop

Flipping me off, Nick smiles
in the mirror, his front
tooth chipped where the shredder
kicked back. Cuff links,
forest green cummerbunds,

everything chosen to match
our dates. *Monkey suits,*
Aunt Starr called them the week
before, handing him a pack of rubbers:
I don't want no grandkids. For days,

we've been mocking
the box, laughing: *lubricant,*
spermicidal. Inside the shop,
mannequins' blank faces stare
from displays, handsome men

in tuxes lean toward us
the way, each spring, cherry trees
bend, crippled by years of pruning,
an answer to ripening heat. I'll kiss—
at prom—Cindy Slater, hoping

Nick will see us, and later
tell the guys in gym
she smells like the science lab.
But today Nick and I help
each other undress, unbuttoning

to reveal a glimpse
of freckled chest, trail of hair
at the waistline. Back at the car,
he laughs, blowing up rubbers
between us, filling them

with his breath. As we drive,
he chucks them one
by one out the window, pale
balloons trailing behind us, mile
after quivering mile.

Omit the Mouth that Answers,

the scrub pine dropping needles in a hush.

Omit the washer junked in the corner, mice making nests in its hose.

Omit his key in the ignition.

Omit exhaust.

Omit the mouth that answers.

Omit the barn cat curled asleep on a pile of kindling in the corner of
the garage.

Omit the bicycle noosed to its rack.

Omit the saw blade's teeth, the workbench hammer, the uncut
plywood beside the rake.

Omit the work lamp with its filmy eye.

Omit his face gone slack.

Omit the mouth that answers.

Omit the algebra book open on the seat.

Omit the moonlight, the cottonwood's glut of hairy seeds.

Omit the drag of the door.

Omit the air let loose from his lungs.

Omit the mouth that answers.

Omit the rise of swallows: wing, beak and claw.

Omit the phone call, the dial tone's skidding hum.

Omit the daylight's questions.

Omit our grieving tongues.

Afterlife

I no longer see him, but the things
he owned see me, snow balling

on the sidewalk like the one
wadded sock he left by the stairs,

a parable in his empty
bottle of Coke, sneakers

still flecked with white paint,
a pair of jeans neatly folded,

grief 's compromise. Months later,
his wadded t-shirt still smells

of chewing tobacco, his basketball jersey
unforgivable in its wrinkled heap.

By the trash can: a drop of blood
where a band aid's tip lies like

a guitar pick, red and gold.
I study the peach pit

still hunkered on the sill, hard eye
watching it all, and ready to bloom.

To the Midwest Wind

Van Buren Street, Columbia City, Indiana

O wonder of rain and weightlessness,
                unroping air wedged with dust
and debris: oak spoor, cotton-fly, cockle-
                bur leaf. Past the mechanic who's fallen
in love today, the whole sky blows
                to motor-grind. Grain husks slide over sun
burnt arms of farm boys, the one
                cop in town holstering his gun.
Dirt, feathers, leaf-rot—everything
                moves: shirts inflating on clotheslines,
tethered sleeves let loose and carried
                over uncut grass where a dropped plum
incandesces to a star. Only bricks,
                scarred with mortar, resist, steady and all
the same; desire, dry heat, and such sudden
                night licking the street lamps into flame.

Closing the Gay Bar Outside Gas City

As if I'd dreamed it up, the front door
still swings, and the dance bell rings
before it dies amid alfalfa, stalks of corn.
On the floor: a faded pair of jeans,
buttons from a shirt. Two condoms
coil like sleepy salamanders
in the back. In Indiana nothing lasts
for long, though here the bathroom lock
still sticks, nourished each winter
by ice and snow. Outside: bones
of rabbits, possum-blur, some ghost's
half-eye through the window screen
where now the only seed that spills is thorny
vine and thistle taking back what's theirs.
Even the magpies, locked in some
blood-sleep, stir in the eaves as if
to speak of patience and regret. Stains
from tossed eggs mar the sides, dents
from stones pitched through windows
boarded up where *FAG* and *AIDS*
are sprayed in flaking paint along
the front. In fifty years, only birds
will couple here. Deer will pause
where a door once opened out to starlight,
locust thorns tearing like some last testament
to beer and lust. Even now, a raccoon
stirs near the window, looks in at me
as it moves past, like some stranger
no longer interested, some boy
who left his lip print on the glass.

Forecast

Today, I'm taking my father
for more tests, his eyes

failing even as we walk
out into the knee deep drifts.

Like his father before,
he takes two shovels from their hooks,

the particles of his hands
sewn somewhere in mine,

so much of him
silent in me as we walk

the bright hemorrhage of white.
He starts at one end,

I start the other, each scoop
unmaking the snow, which has taken

over porches, stoops, skeletal trees
hedging the road. Soon,

he won't be able to make out the handle
he's gripping. We don't speak,

piling the crude heaps,
first him, then me, the black

grammar of railroad ties
announcing the perimeter.

The weatherman calls for more—
seven inches by nightfall—

but the old Chevy rattles
as I rev the engine,

my father leaning to scrape
the windshield clear of ice

until he's certain I can see.

Lantern Light, Big Cedar

Into their depths anything could vanish:
old tractor tires, crooked limbs
from a tree. They stitched the county—
Blue Lake, Goose Lake, Big Cedar—
carved by the ancient glacier, Nick said,
that once claimed half the state.
Some were 100 feet deep. Others, I imagined,
went on forever, crystalline, refracting light.
On land I could feel them lap against me
as if I was the boat my uncle made
from oak the lightening struck. That June
he'd run off with a hairdresser from Muncie.
Aunt Starr cried for weeks, watching us
slit bluegill, tease out each bone, white
meat heaped on torn newspaper. *Watch out,*
she said, *for the blood suckers,* taking her
cigarette to a black leech on my calf.
At night in the basement, Nick lay beside me:
light on bare arms, fumbling that grew
furious as the mulberry bloomed outside
the basement window. I wanted to believe
he could take my hand and change me forever
while the kitchen plumbing gurgled over our heads
and the electric meter ticked on the damp
limestone wall. I wanted to believe
we could vanish along the fault line
between our fear and the reservoir,
whose water fed Big Cedar, carrying the vast
loneliness of the deep. Some nights
we took the boat into Blank Cove,
crouched at the bucket's rim over a knot
of speared Pike, fresh wounds gripping their sides.
Once we saw a dead Lab heaped on the shore,
milky-eyed and toothless, a riot of flies
in its head. We knew that's how a body rose

after days in water, incandescent in lantern light,
sopping fur tangled in weeds. Drifting,
I leaned on his chest gone hollow
as the old cedar trunk where the neighbor kids hid
when their mothers called them in at dusk.
I felt his veins pumping, hands shiny
with fish guts, those eyes that closed when he pressed
against me in the basement, sewn into my sleep.
Sometimes we didn't care to remember
the way back home, taking the open lake
toward the lone pines following each other
up the hill, but always, we turned around,
emptying our nets at the creaking pier, touching
the cool, slick bodies—eyes, gills, fins—
our faces still locked in each wave, floating
and not floating, again and again.

Afterlife

The pine he stripped of bark goes grey
at the edges. When I stop, everything

is here again: the half-tune of our
breath, his raft-like stretch of chest, shore

wrecked by flooding. I hear him say
my name in full as if taking me whole

in his mouth, jack pine shaking,
needles dark with our breathing,

each cobweb's shadow really a body
listening, unwilling to miss anything.

Paradise, Indiana

Some nights the streets divided me
       like one of those snowy Indiana towns

with names like *Paradise* or *Liberty,*
       the Kankakee sweeping its icy waters

past the winter carnival rising into the dark.
       This was the stuff, they claimed, God made

us for: the whole town rumbling
       with the smell of sweet ribs, the slaughter

house sprawling under angels
       with plastic wings, a blow-up Santa.

Crowds gathered at the ticket booth,
       a hog turning on its spit. My father

coughed a lit Camel through the cracked window,
       Mom in the front seat, the whole car shaking

as they fought near the barbecue pit, love
       unfolding its smoke and ash. It never ended,

that road back home past The Church of God
       where the preacher said we'd one day rise

whole-bodied into the sky, the graveyard
       frozen thick with children from

the cholera epidemic of 1906. I could feel
       the sky crush down on me in the dead

of winter, but some mornings the fields
       were so vast in their whiteness that the silos

towered like the future, ice-caked and glistening.
        I'd put my frozen hands in my pockets

to keep them warm or watch my parents
        walking arm in arm past the nativity

with its Baby Jesus, twice stolen, now nailed
        to the manger, his cracked halo painted so yellow

it could be, if seen from a distance, polished gold.

The Death of the Avon Lady

As a boy, I watched you
on our sofa spreading powders
    and honey soaps, your satchel
open to perfumes, lipsticks, hopes

    embodied in the names:
Surrender, Sin, Always Tomorrow.
    My mother changed
diapers, scrubbed cat piss

    from rugs on hands and knees,
but you drifted in the door,
    bright red nails and shapely calves.
I remember how you leaned

    and touched my face
and, once, you winked. But now
    the hillside holds you, dark
hair fanning in the crush

    of green, the whole ridge
soft and feminine, scent
    of lavender, sage, jewels of sap
from sweet gum pods

    splitting open like the small
tumors in your breast.
    Already death seems different,
the way the hawk preens

    the field mouse in its jaws,
the way the hillside
    turns luminous as its ribs
crack apart. For days I watch

a cabbage rose moving
sunward and ravenous, gone
gorgeous in its foul
disintegrating heart.

Heat Lightning Over Tunker

This time of year the suicides go up,
July's inferno, aphid-hell, cutworms
and scale; power sprayer making a fuss
over fingerlings, lime sulfur fog and Paris Green.
Everything inside you moves like deer

rubbing antler buds on the tree bark.
The sun blurs to trick the eyes. Shed paint
peels like a nicotine patch. Across the road
a barn door slams where the first boy you kissed
got down on his knees, the heat conjuring his hands,

his shameful mouth. Antler horns screw
into your bedroom wall, sweat stains
spreading out beyond corn fields gorged
on road kill and seed. How have you come
to live where pigs rub their muddy snouts

on the trough and the ruffed grouse
impales itself on a hackberry thorn? Today,
you're the burr on the raccoon's leg,
the squeaking cemetery gate. Again, you move
past wordlessness where creek beds unravel

like the barn dog's wormy heart. So much
vanishes down the road that takes you home
to the lakeside graveyard on the hill
with its crumbling headstones caked
in moss and cattail fuzz, crawdads wandering

the caretaker's shed. Here, the dead
know better than to ask for much:
mound of dirt, pine box. On the shore
there's just another old fishing boat,
but it's more than enough to cross.

The Girlfriend

She calls him *Nicky.*
She twirls her hair with one finger.
When she gets a crucifix ankle-tattoo,
she says, *It's for Jesus.*
When she gets a B in geometry,
she cries. In her father's apartment
above the filling station, the smell of oil rags
mixes with the tangerine lotion
she rubs on her legs.
At the wake, everyone
will say how hard it is to watch her
stand with Aunt Starr,
weeping over the casket.
She'll collapse outside the funeral home,
then speak at the school memorial,
wearing a bracelet
she's woven from his hair.
Teachers will shake their heads:
such a tragedy for a young girl.
That spring, she'll date a guy
on the basketball team.
Drinking Boone's, they'll park
at Millford's Quarry, cranking
the radio in her brother's truck.
They'll talk for hours.
They'll make out.
When I pass her at school,
I'll pretend I don't see her.
Along route 9, corn will rise again in the fields.
The leaves will bud as they always bud.
After the rains,
tent caterpillars will fill the trees like snow.
Webbed and resinous, they'll cover
entire limbs, multiplying as they feed,

a strange white silence
even kerosene can't kill.

Fortress

After his death, Aunt Starr disappeared
in heaps of faux gold jewelry, a river
of coffee pots and purses, spare light
bulbs, Bible verses. She wrote scripture
on seed catalogues, prayed to
the God of another spatula, another
sponge, ten lawn mower blades
and her sudden lunge for the thrift
store bin. She stored potatoes on top
of apple cores, Reba McEntire
records and the penny jar. Her dogs
pissed on the floor, fouled
the recliner. Penciling one eyebrow,
she forgot the other. She ate,
in bed, her poppy-seed cakes,
came to Christmas with lard
on her shirt. Eighteen oven timers,
a dozen brooms, nine silver
vacuums made a misshapen
fortress in his room where
she now slept alone, dreaming of her
thirteen crock pots simmering
meat and broth and bone.

Credo

I believe in his foot hitting the accelerator.

I believe in the traffic light, its green fuse over every street.

I believe in cows hemmed in by rain and milk.

The secret places we go: old Yoder Road, lots behind the gutted saw mill.

Heaven, Nick jokes, is the back of his car.

I believe ephemerals.

Turnips push, radishes root down.

I believe the cracked mount nurses the oil leak, steady shiver in the light.

I believe in creek, corn and sycamore, vastness broken where thorns unwind.

I believe in the lake, turtles tucked in burrows, their drowsing three-chambered hearts.

I believe our hands in the icy water. I'm a kid, and then I'm not.

I believe in the crumbling elm, which owes nothing to memory.

Let the loons lift. Let the past recede into rapeseed.

Faith is the shrinking distance between his mouth and mine.

I believe the fate of the shoreline.

I believe cattails shattering into seed.

Nothing can stop the waves.

Let the fish strain against fish lines.

Let the bloody pliers tear out the hooks.

To Interstate 70

Wheat fields, white lines, everything
        blurs—*Hazelwood, Spring Grove, Clover*

Dale fractured in the VW's headlights.
        Though the exit ramp promises

escape, the solid yellow line resists
        the crossing over. Cornfields interrupt

the hard beauty of the gas pumps,
        the gleaming *Conocos* of the heart-

land rising where road kill opens
        to reveal what shines. Semis awaken

the muddied green, lumber hauled
        from *Terre Haute*—walnut, black oak,

butternut and pine—the whole state
        tied to the wheel in the vague landscape

of travel: a man in a red truck, a woman's
        radio blaring, so many strangers passing

in separate zones, even the lonely
        going nowhere, and arriving home.

On the Road to Goshen

Driven off road by storm, Mom and I
took shelter in the Kroger Store, water-
melons corded by the door,

a TV on the stand flashing
sand bags and the Coast Guard
called out. The river rose,

homes swept whole down
the riverbank, graveyards submerged,
the dead drifting watery rooms, carp

in sock drawers, clocks gurgling
on walls, a table floating with its bowl
of peaches. The TV flickered. News

and more news: four bodies washed up
at the Church of God near its sign:
And The Lord was sorry He had

made man on the earth. Outside,
rain slowed over toppled
grocery carts, plastic bags guttering

hail-starred window shields, the end
sudden as the beginning, blood
that washed us clean. We walked—

when the waters receded—
from store to home, Mom
saying rosary for twin boys drowned

in their attic, just a mile from
where I'd been born. *Hail Mary,*
she said as thick mud

took our feet, and empty
field rows oozed with
the coming memory of corn.

Afterlife

A new thing, this silence
between us—his headstone rising

inarticulate from dirt. I listen:
a squirrel chatters near the creek bed.

His memory, an endless window
I can't get shut. I wake to cold nights,

sleep all day. I dream the car,
salvage sign swinging over its hard face.

I touch the door, windshield gone
and everything revealed: torn seats

and the stink of gasoline, blackbirds
on the dash where his head lay,

each dropped seed picked clean.

Vows

Tonight love is a paper tablecloth,
cold cuts fanned on a tray.
We weave through dancing couples,
cousin Doris—the bride—hovering
over squares of cheese.
When no one is looking, we drink from the keg.
By the sheet cake, his girlfriend
scans the crowd.
I pull him out back.
In Uncle Duffy's truck bed, we sit,
drinking flat beer from a two-liter.
He holds two half-smoked cigarettes,
snug caterpillars in his palm.
From inside: muffled bluegrass.
Nick strikes a match, leans close,
forehead peeling from too much sun.
We smoke and drink. In the pasture,
cows drool green in a lather of gnats.
Onion maggots tunnel bulb and crown.
Feeding, they work through the night.
I write my name on his hand.
He laughs. We're drunk.
Anything we say can be taken back.
He leans against me. I push him
down, spilling beer on his shirt.
He says, *We shouldn't.*
He says, *Unbuckle your belt.*
I imagine he keeps his eyes open.
When we rise, the world is different,
a split Hefty bag dumped by the roadside,
night's code of milk cartons and rancid meat.
Departing couples walk through the lot.
His girlfriend, dragging her purse, appears:
Where have you been? When I say
his name, he doesn't answer.

Climbing into his car,
they peel out toward route 9
where they'll pass the Dairy Queen,
then the butcher shop, a bag
of cow hearts stacked in its display.
It's August. Hot. From the gravel drive,
I watch him turn the corner,
wind curling his hair. Dogs bark
in the distance. An owl rises.
The hard dust of his passage reddens the air.

The Ambiguity of Stone

I want to believe the last time
I saw him no language was needed
between us, a dive lure flaring
like a tiny orange flame between rubber
night crawlers as a breath from
my mouth entered his. Frost had
taken the ground the week
before. Everything seemed ready
to harden or split wide, tractor parts
lodged in stiff dirt, the mulberry's
sap clogged by cold. Even now,
I want to believe eternity exists
in that corner of the lake where we once
saw Bobby Gary take a BB in the eye,
where cattails forked in summer,
and on our last afternoon Nick leaned
to bait his hook. A week later,
he'd be dead. In the woods
I'd find a bike so honeycombed
with hornet nests I could taste
their wings in my chest. The whole sky
would quiver, power lines cross-
hatching clouds as if someone had
stitched them with a lightening hum.
But that last day, everything
went quiet. Pounding out dents
in the shanty, we talked of smallmouth jigs
and where the bluegills might bed
in the spring. We cast our lines,
gutting a trout that spilled its clutch
of eggs, until the last sun sank
over us the way it sinks over
quarry stone ready to be made
into church steps or garden statuary,
so that even as we packed up our things,

something inside him waited
to emerge as a flock of starlings
made a shadow of his face, the cold
night swallowing old row boats
on a shoreline it had already erased.

Cruising the Rest Stop on Route 9

From where you stand you can feel
the back road empty into the county,
an endless need. Moths flicker
at the bulb's lit nerve, coupling

and uncoupling over greasy linoleum.
You lean against the sink, its faucet
dripping, trying to form a word, night
stalled between hand and zipper.

You know a man on his knees
can read the scored tile, torque of
his mouth filled with night and the marsh
fields' dampness. Anything can happen

when the urinal flushes, but tonight
the trucker won't look up. That's how
it is sometimes, paper towels clogging
the drainpipe, water blackened with rust.

Outside, cars deliver strangers
past orchards where raccoons poach
rotting plums from low cracked limbs,
all that sweet flesh waking in the dark.

The Afterlife of Roadkill

See the brown mutt bleed through
its garland of burrs, a torn
possum drooling dried streaks
of foam, lice-flecked raccoons

on the yellow line, split wide.
See how wholly they open to us
in death, to the moon, to the red elm
scabbed with mites. They open

to riverbeds and the song
of the wren, to flowering plums
and the barbed wire fence. Over
and over they open to carrion

birds catching scent, beginning
to rise. Even their skulls,
picked clean, look upwards, knowing
nothing of their missing eyes.

The Smoke

Past houses, past pickers and bone-cleaners,
       rats and carrion birds, alley cats clawing

out fish heads from the trash, the smoke
       rose, a black river shivering. It rose

past Churubusco and Wawasee, Goose Lake
       and Big Cedar, past the steer calf

grinding its bud-teeth, and the dogs
       that stopped barking to sniff the air.

As it traveled, it carried the boy
       who started it all, flames climbing

his sleeve to his collar to the baseball cap
       dazzling now on his head. It carried

his screams past the gutted warehouse,
       past *Max's Metal, Iron & Scrap.* It rose

into combines, filling the dead machines.
       One hair at a time, it rose with his waxen

face, eyes and skin spilling into weather,
       fields, crops, the peach trees withering,

fruit darkened, maggot at the root.
       It rose where nothing else could:

into attic crevices, into dreams of people
       sleeping in their beds. It blackened

the steps of the Baptist Church
       where later the congregation would pray

for the match struck just to watch it flare
      in the darkness, for the way a body is lifted

smoking from the grass, for the trees—
      how they flickered outside the window—

for all that would be remembered:
      the dirt road's grieving, the harvest time,

the sewing of the seeds, for the season
      they knew would follow through Autumn's

blazing maples, through the poplar and ash.

Indiana History

I hate the textbook and its answers, Mr. Webber and his questions.

Indiana, meaning "Indian Land," becomes the nineteenth state,
December 11, 1816.

Never touch the face, says the mortician. Never tip the casket when
you lift.

I study but remember it wrong.

Who was the Klan's most powerful leader?

Photos of men hanging limp, bare feet dangling.

Mr. Webber labels *Eel, White, Tippecanoe.*

Even Nick's hands seem smaller, cheeks rouged, mouth not quite his.

Even my Father sobs, Aunt Starr taking him by the arm.

General Harrison slaughters natives at Prophettown, scorched heads
driven onto poles.

Mr. Webber writes *bison and elk, tools of shell and stone.*

*During the 1920s, Indiana became the stronghold of a national hate
group.*

Suddenly so many flowers, the fact of the dead body fogs the room.

Grandma mixes nuts in the white bowl: *Brazil nuts, almonds.*

She taps their shells with a ball-head hammer, cracks the *nigger-toes.*

The jack pine scrapes the parlor window.

I study but remember it wrong.

I want to crawl in beside him, feel his chest, the cold slope of his
　　　pelvis.

Mr. Webber says: *Questions?*

The jack pine casts its black seeds to the earth.

Afterlife

It takes both hands to unfix the spike
he drove into the fence post, worrying dirt
loose from around its base. A spider spins
the ache in my throat. If he were here,

what would he be doing? I torch a phonebook,
watching the names and numbers burn.
I feel the fallen phone line, the horned lark
crushed in the mailbox's rusty throat.

Weevils become the dream work of fields,
the old shack set back in the tree line.
I'm tired of the corn, their fibrous heads.
I'm tired of the white cocoon in the old jam jar,

the fruit bat brimming with darkness.
Barbed wire, concrete slab, slag in the rusty water.
I walk the yard of Holsteins, dewlaps quivering,
nerves pulsing in the udders. Two miles away

the Wal-Mart is going in, barns giving way
to Pizza Hut, Penguin Point. I look across
the silent field. The plow is hard. My heart
is hard. Dirt. Distance. It does not end.

Someone Knocks on a Door in the State Where I Was Born

Take me back where hag moths feed
on sweet gums, threshers crushing

wild grapes. Where fields curb
the slaughterhouse, tractors weighted

with wheat. Take me where cars
feed turnpikes, and bones break

down in their graves. Where roads pass
smokestacks; steel pipes scored on the lathe.

Apricots sleep inside branches
as the hunters slip deep into spring.

And a hog drowns in the culvert.
And the muskrat gives over its skin.

Where dirt calls to the ash roots,
the screech owl calling to rain.

Where a boy leans on a headstone,
pretending not to hear his name.

Lure

Muskrats enter the trap
for the apple, the lure

we've secured with a nail.
They can't be saved,

nesting the banks, cloudy-
eyed, whiskered hunger

deep as our own. They
mate and breed. Where they die

in the cold: frogs, crayfish
gleam, cattail roots, scat

steaming. We lift them—
seven dollars a pelt—

into the boat, fur matted, legs
cage-snagged as if punished

for feeding. Into water
they come rippling,

immeasurable. Where
it begins. Where it ends.

That feeling. So many names:
mud cat, mud beaver, heart-

stopped in the rushes, snared.

Gutting the White-Tail

Having shot it, we must clean it.
We are shaking
with our good fortune.
Our hands numb from cold,
we roll the carcass onto its back.
The belly is soft.
It is snowing.
We've never done this before,
but we've seen it done.
While I spread the hind legs,
Nick cuts breastbone to tail.
Like butter, he jokes,
moving slowly, avoiding the paunch and intestines,
holding them away from the knife.
Ok, he says, *Why did the farmer*
name his pig "Ink"?
He slits around the anus,
drawing it up into the body.
Why? I ask.
He imitates a drum roll:
It kept running out of the pen.
Gathering the ropy mass,
he rolls the stomach out onto the frozen ground.
The rest comes quickly:
liver, diaphragm, the pelvic bone's
quick crack. With a heave,
he splits the breast, pulling gullet, lungs, heart.
By now he's out of breath.
We flip the body belly down.
Blood pools,
spreading out like roads on a map.
We know not to break the bladder.
We know how quickly the intestines sour.
We high-five, passing a cigarette as the body cools.
We are alone together.

He is alive.
We watch the windpipe steaming in the snow.

About the Author

Bruce Snider s the author of *The Year We Studied Women* (2003), which won the Felix Pollack Poery Prize from the University of Wisconsin Press. A former Wallace Stegner Fellow and the recipient of a James A. Michener fellowship, Snider lives in San Francisco and currently teaches at the University of San Francisco.

Poems in this collection previously appeared in:

Bellingham Review: "Heat Lightning Over Tunker," "Parts," "Omit the Mouth that Answers"

Cimarron Review: "Lantern Light, Big Cedar"

Crazyhorse: "At These Speeds," "At the Midwest Taxidermy Convention"

EDNA: "Afterlife" ("I no longer see him but the things") under the title "Mourning"

The Florida Review: "To the Midwest Wind" under the title "Ode to the Midwest Wind"

The Gettysburg Review: "The Drag Queen Dies in New Castle"

Linebreak: "The Smoke"

Massachusetts Review: "Afterlife" ("The cold day grinds like a starter") under the title "Mourning I"

Meridian: "Late Harvest," "Romance"

Nimrod: "The Ambiguity of Stone"

Ninth Letter: "A Great Whirring," "Lure," "Chemistry"

Notre Dame Review: "Planetary"

Pleiades: "Closing the Gay Bar Outside Gas City," "Tornado Season," "Forecast"

Ploughshares: "Epitaph"

RATTLE: "Cruising the Rest Stop on Route 9"

Sycamore Review: "Paradise, Indiana"

"The Drag Queen Dies in New Castle" was reprinted in *The Best American Poetry 2012,* edited by Mark Doty and David Lehman.

"A Great Whirring" was reprinted on Verse Daily.

"Forecast" and "To Interstate 70" received a 2011 Dorothy Sargent Rosenberg Poetry Prize.

Acknowledgements

For support during the writing of this book, thanks goes to Stanford University's Wallace Stegner Program, the James A. Michener Center for Writers at The University of Texas at Austin, the James Merrill House and the Merrill House Committee, the Amy Clampitt House and the Berkshire Taconic Foundation, and the Millay Colony for the Arts.

Thanks to all my colleagues at Stanford University and to friends and teachers who provided indispensable help, editorial and otherwise: Marla Akin, Eavan Boland, Lynn and Jeff Callahan, Beth Chapoton, Simone DiPiero, Robin and Keith Ekiss, Ken Fields, Maria Hummel, Amaud Johnson, Tom Kealey, Jim Magnuson, Mike McGriff, Sara Michas-Martin, Brian Mikesell, Mary Popek, Doug Powell, Steven Rahe, David Roderick, Brian Spears, and TJ Wasden.

Thanks to Alice Friman for choosing the book, to Wayne Miller for his thoughtful and generous editorial skills, and to everyone at Pleiades Press and Louisiana State University Press for their outstanding work and commitment.

Thanks to my family for their support and patience with all of my questions.

Very special thanks to Shara Lessley for her unrivaled friendship, ruthless editorial eye, and for holding my hand through it all. This book wouldn't exist without you.

And finally my endless gratitude to Lysley, who gave this wandering Hoosier a home.

Also Available from Pleiades Press

Landscape with Headless Mama by Jennifer Givhan

Random Exorcisms by Adrian C. Louis

Poetry Comics from the Book of Hours by Bianca Stone

The Belle Mar by Katie Bickham

Sylph by Abigail Cloud

The Glacier's Wake by Katy Didden

Paradise, Indiana by Bruce Snider

What's this, Bombadier? by Ryan Flaherty

Self-Portrait with Expletives by Kevin Clark

Pacific Shooter by Susan Parr

It was a terrible cloud at twilight by Alessandra Lynch

Compulsions of Silkworms & Bees by Julianna Baggott

Snow House by Brian Swann

Motherhouse by Kathleen Jesme

Lure by Nil Michals

The Green Girls by John Blair

A Sacrificial Zinc by Matthew Cooperman

The Light in Our House by Al Maginnes

Strange Wood by Kevin Prufer

PLEIADES
P R E S S